T0288093

NOMADIC PRESS

OAKLAND

111 FAIRMONT AVENUE
OAKLAND, CA 94611

BROOKLYN

475 KENT AVENUE #302
BROOKLYN, NY 11249

WWW.NOMADICPRESS.ORG

MASTHEAD

FOUNDING AND MANAGING EDITOR
J. K. FOWLER

ASSOCIATE EDITOR
MICHAELA MULLIN

DESIGN
BRITTA FITHIAN-ZURN

MISSION STATEMENT

Through publications, events, and active community participation, Nomadic Press collectively weaves together platforms for intentionally marginalized voices to take their rightful place within the world of the written and spoken word. Through our limited means, we are simply attempting to help right the centuries' old violence and silencing that should never have occurred in the first place and build alliances and community partnerships with others who share a collective vision for a future far better than today.

SUBMISSIONS

Nomadic Press wholeheartedly accepts unsolicited book manuscripts during its open reading period every year. To submit your work, please visit: www.nomadicpress.org/submissions

DISTRIBUTION

Orders by trade bookstores and wholesalers:
Small Press Distribution,
1341 Seventh Street
Berkeley, CA 94701
spd@spdbooks.org
(510) 524-1668 / (800) 869-7553

This book was made possible by a loving community of chosen family and friends, old and new.

For author questions or to book a reading at your bookstore, university/school, or alternative establishment, please send an email to info@nomadicpress.org.

Cover artwork by Conn Ryder (connryder.com)

Published by Nomadic Press, 111 Fairmount Avenue, Oakland, CA 94611

First printing, 2019

Library of Congress Cataloging-in-Publication Data

Title: *this is my body*

p. cm.

Summary: *this is my body* is an anthology of written works by women of color exploring their relationship with their bodies in the world they exist in. Each piece is accompanied by a QR code link to a powerful stage performance bringing the words from the page to life.

[1. Women. 2. Bodies. 3. American General.] I. III. Title.

ISBN: 978-1-732786646

this is my body

WOMEN OF COLOR RECLAIMING NARRATIVES OF SELF AND BODY

KIERA A. | BRITTANY RAE BUCKMIRE
LULU CHENG | BRITTNEY ENIN
LAUREN ITO | MADIHA KHAN
SHEMIKA LAMARE | SARAH D. PARK
JADE-OLIVIA PATTON | MAREKO PRIOR

EDITORS VINA VO AND ODELIA YOUNGE

this is my body

WOMEN OF COLOR RECLAIMING
NARRATIVES OF SELF AND BODY

NOMADIC
PRESS

TO ALL THE WOMEN WHO HAVE NURTURED
STORIES IN US. MAY WE CONTINUE
TO BREATHE LIFE INTO THEM.

CONTENTS

FOREWORD

On October 15, 2017, the digital reemergence of the #MeToo movement overwhelmed our timelines and our testimonies. With the innumerable posts of women bearing witness to the pain and trauma of their encounters with sexual harassment and assault, the ramifications of toxic masculinity, pervasive patriarchy, and male sexual violence were unmistakable.

For millennia, women's bodies have been objectified by men who crafted social conditions steeped in sexism, misogyny, and misogynoir.[1] For women of color, particularly Black women, gendered oppression is compounded due to its inextricable links to issues of class and status. From the highest office on US soil to congressional hearings, women's bodies are literally under attack. Whether it is a travel ban on our Islamic sisters or an abortion ban eliminating safe access for pregnancy termination, federal and state governments are doing all they can to take us back to a society that is a warped mix of chattel slavery and *The Handmaiden's Tale*.

When Odelia and Vina, co-founders of the Novalia Collective asked me to be a mentor for the inaugural cohort of *this is my body* performers, I relished the opportunity to be a part of an intentionally women/womxn-centric production. *this is my body* is more than a program; it is a journey into hearts, minds, and yes, even bodies, of women who are using narrative as resistance.

From bodily functions to surgery, and rape to domestic violence, these women storytellers (none of them self identified as performers) conveyed personal narratives that still had collective impact. It was as if their stories were our stories and they offered us a composite of everywoman. And, no matter how one identifies in terms of pronouns, everyone can relate to vulnerability. It is our transparency that will save us.

1"Misogynoir" is a term coined by Moya Bailey to describe the dual nature of oppression Black women face living at the intersection of race and gender.

In order to show up fully in the world, however, we must carve out safe, protected space for the most marginalized voices among us. This lack of oral/aural sanctuary is why I founded beautiful scars, an online storytelling agency focused on trauma, healing, and resiliency. Our first campaign, #WereSurthrivors,[2] was created for Black Christian women who have suffered childhood sexual abuse and/or male sexual violence. By harnessing the power of narrative, I aim aiding individuals and communities to shift from silence to storytelling to put an end to gender-based violence, for good.

Novalia Collective has defined a communal space that coaxes participants to co-create a new heaven and a new earth through the gift of breaking open their lives for the consumption of the masses. Art is resistance. And Self-Love is art. As women continue to defy social norms and engage in radical Self-acceptance, Self-compassion, and Self-adoration, we continue to deconstruct, destroy, and eradicate the world's sinful bigotry and xenophobia.

Statistics don't change people—stories do. I invite you to bear witness to these stories. Savor them. Share them. Honor them. Believe them. Fight for the liberation of all women. Utilize your position of power to create platforms for women's voices. Use your privilege to amplify women's voices. Lobby to protect women's agency over their own bodies. Hire women. Cite women. Fund women. Love women.

Odelia and Vina are in alignment with this era of the rise of divine feminine energy. The words you are holding are precious. They have been to the darkest corners and are finally squinting into the light. These words have been thoughtfully curated to include a spectrum of women's experiences that, as first-person narratives, are bound together as a sacred text.

Read their words. Hear their hearts. Let their stories sink into your very being.

And then, go out and tell your own.

LYVONNE PROVERBS, MDIV
FOUNDER, BEAUTIFUL SCARS

---

2   "Surthrivor" is a term I coined in 2009 when, as a victim of father-daughter incest and intimate partner violence, the term "survivor" did not resonate with me. I was in seminary, had deep community, and was thriving. "Surthrivor:" one who has flourished despite facing life's harsh extenuating circumstances.

Lyvonne Proverbs, MDiv is a body and sex-positive pastor and consultant working to end #ChurchToo and the founder of beautiful scars (@WereSurthrivors), an online storytelling agency focused on trauma, healing, and resiliency. You can follow her @LyvonneP.

INTRODUCTION

THE POWER OF STORY

We are the daughters of refugees and immigrants. The children of the margins and migrations. We first met each other working in education. We couldn't tell you the exact moment we met. All we know is that the first encounter was a grand gift of the universe. We were drawn together by the power of stories.

Our families have strong oral-history traditions. It's how we have mapped our existence on this earth and the spaces we have cultivated into homes. They document our survival, our narratives. We know ourselves through these stories. We grow strong in their truths.

Over the years, as women of color, these stories have been a source of emotional, physical, and spiritual survival and thriving. We witnessed this in one another, but recognized that too often women's—and especially women of color—stories remained lodged inside of them. While silencing us, our worlds have also taught us to silence ourselves.

Breaking the silence of oppression has transformed both our lives. We wanted to find others to share that with. We wanted to help birth stories—stories for ourselves and for our communities.

OUR WORK

It isn't just the power of story, but also its promise that guides our work. Vulnerable storytelling asks us to believe in the promise before we see the power. The promise of healing and connection. The promise that we can imagine anew.

We are living in the wake of #MeToo. A time of anger and backlash and war waged against women and our bodies. But our stories as women began long before the traumatic events that have been exposed through #MeToo.

We are the culmination of all of the smaller moments when we were told how to dress, when to talk, were spoken over, spoken for, taught to endure levels of pain and humiliation, and made to draw into ourselves and not cause "trouble." Our lives, our bodies, have been everyone's but our own. *this is my body*, like all of our work, has been about owning our own narratives in a way that does not erase the stories that have existed and exist, but rather allows us to name them for ourselves.

this is my body

this is my body began as a personal project for the two of us to engage with the one-woman genre through the lens of a specific theme. But we quickly remembered our desire to share in the powerful nature of storytelling with others, and imagined what it would be like to support women through the process of developing a shorter-length, one-woman show. When thinking of a theme, it did not take Odelia long to decide on "this is my body"— a rallying cry of self determination based on her personal experiences. From there, we developed *this is my body* as a program which consisted of supporting a group of amateur women-identifying storytellers through the journey of taking an idea for a story to the development of an original 5-minute, one-woman show. We did this through a series of writing and performance workshops grounded in vulnerable storytelling, self-exploration, and community. While our implementation of the program has continued to shift and grow, it remains grounded in these values. For three-and-a-half months, our authors and performers came together as a collective that helped each of them dive deep into their stories and come away with pieces that articulated an important story in their life.

Some of the women whose stories you will read as part of this anthology identify as writers and others do not. And they are all creators because they have all whispered a story into the air and grabbed tightly to it until it manifested in the words on the pages before you. Some of the stories you will witness in this anthology are stories that have never been shared before; stories that required immense vulnerability and reflection to extract, and courage to deliver. The stories you will read are scripts of their performance which you can also watch by scanning the QR code on each page.

As performances go, the words captured on the page might not exactly match the words shared on stage. That's part of the beauty of storytelling: to liberate yourself from the page and let the moment take over. Although we did edit this anthology for formatting, we retained the style and voice of each author to celebrate the diverse ways in which we communicate and tell stories. To witness the joy, healing, and transformation that came from the organic love and care that our authors had for one another was an inspiring gift—to see their brilliance encapsulated on stage to a crowd of strangers and friends was even greater.

THE FUTURE

It is hard to quantify how *this is my body* has shown up in the lives of the women who have been part of the program and in our own lives. We know that it has challenged all of us. We know that it has called us into deep community with one another, and has given us space and time to define parts of ourselves.

This show truly started with Odelia's fervent belief that if you send your intentions into the universe, the right resources and people will come. As such, we are continuing with this tried-and-true tradition by sending our intentions into the hands of the readers of this anthology. Our vision is for *this is my body* to expand to other regions outside of the Bay to continue to elevate the voices of those who are ready to reclaim space and have their voices heard.

We hope that you will savor these stories and allow them to find ways into your world of understanding and that you may see bits of yourself in ways you never imagined possible. If these stories and performances impact you in any way, share them with someone else so that they too may feel heard, seen, and understood.

VINA VO AND ODELIA YOUNGE
CO-FOUNDERS, NOVALIA COLLECTIVE

BRITTNEY ENIN

Writing about the ways that I am in love with myself brings me joy. It was my first time writing about how an aspect of my body (my Beauty Gap in my teeth) serves as a conduit for connecting me, and others around me, to the spiritual and ancestral power that comprises the reservoirs of radical sunshine and wisdom that I manifest daily in my life. It also feels good as a young Black woman in her 20s, post-college, to be able to slow down and reflect on aspects of my existence that I did not have the emotional space to process earlier in my life. It was also my first time centering my identity as a daughter of African immigrants and being able to comfortably talk about the ways in which I experience my particular brand of Blackness, and the struggle to remain steadfast and connected to my cultural knowledge even though I am not on my ancestral land. Most of all, this piece represents the way that I treasure the things that make me different, and how I don't care about what people think of my Fat, Black body, with Gaps in my teeth. I feel free in loving me.

**SCAN TO
WATCH A LIVE
PERFORMANCE
OF THE PIECE.**

BEAUTY GAP

In my 24th Suncycle of life, telling stories about my body is an act that comes with the clarity of Retrospective Reflection. 'Cause up until the Lord walked into my life, I didn't know what it was like to be in my body; I only knew how to exist and survive. Now that I am in a place of Thriving, I have the soulspace to appreciate the totality of my physical self that has gotten me this far in this beautiful, yet broken, society. My story to tell today is about my teeth.

I created the Gap between my two front teeth. For 14 years, I sucked on my index and middle fingers on my right hand. My milk teeth shifted to lay a way for the permanent placing of my long-term teeth whose top and bottom rows would never touch. I don't regret my actions. The finger sucking was my way of coping with the rumbling of my tummy that reflected the Black hole Darkness of the empty kitchen cupboard.

This is the first lesson my Gap taught me: *learning how to be full on space.*

During the holiday gatherings with my extended family, spending time amidst the aromas of peanut butter soup and jollof rice filling my lungs, my joyful smile was regarded by my Ghanaian elders: "Your smile is so beautiful! The Gap in your teeth means you are pretty in our Ghanaian culture!"

I was in awe as they told me that my Beauty Gap also signified intelligence (this is why I was such a straight-A student, I thought!). Looking back on my preteens, I realized how much I thirsted for Homeland Acceptance, being a first-gen Ghanaian American.

This is the second lesson my beauty gap revealed to me: *the gap between my Ghanaian Ancestry and American Reality.*

Nevertheless, learning this ancestral truth taught me that I never have to question my intelligence and my beauty because my ancestors never did. Returning to school the following Monday, I found myself pitying the metallic mouths of my middle school, middle-class peers, pushing through the pain of wearing braces day after day, striving for the straight teeth of the American Mainstream. "Thank God I never have to do that!"

Or so I thought.

On the 30th year of my mom's immigration to America and my senior year of college, my mom gave me her advice to help me get ready to enter the adult world: "You need to get braces and close your gap when you get a high-paying job with your degree. People make judgments about the way you look, and can take away opportunity if you don't look like an American."

There was no questioning her words. After all, she came to this country with nothing and only has her children to show for her efforts. My financial success is her survival, and I would do anything to make sure she and I could leave the vestiges of American poverty.

Upon my graduation and entry into white-collar employment, I planned to use my newly gotten dental insurance to achieve the American Dream bestowed upon me. I was going to close my Gap and become a middle-class "professional."

Then, my ancestors intervened.

Two months into my new job, I participated in a racial-equity training. I walked into a room with chairs arranged in a big circle with both melanated and non-melanated colleagues filling them in. The topic of discussion was internalized racism. I took my seat, confident that there was going to be more learning done by the "snowflake people" than I did. A handout was passed around and it was labeled "Internalized Racism Inventory," and I looked at example #7 which stated: *"Do I intend to alter my physical features in any way to hide or obscure my own cultural or ethnic features?"*

I gasped in horror at the "yes" echoing in my body. I was intending to bind my teeth with metal ropes like the British used rope to bind my ancestors to captivity. I was going to throw away my Gap-toothed heritage for White Supremacist acceptance that would never be mine, 'cause I am still Black, Fat, and a Woman. *Whoo!*

My ancestors spoke through the wisdom present in my renewed commitment to preserving my Gap Teeth, teaching me my final lesson: *loving yourself will never come from chasing the ideals in a society that was not built to understand your majesty.*

When I went home that night, humbled and grateful, I looked at myself in the mirror, and smiled to greet and apologize to my Beauty Gap that I had taken for granted and almost erased. Suddenly, I saw light wash over me; radiance casting out the darkness of the classist, white supremacist standards of beauty that had hold over my life.

When I smile so confident and unashamed, the grace, love, and compassion I have for those around me emerges; the Beauty and support of my Ghanaian Ancestors rebuking the negativity of those who don't love their imperfections; the joyful laughter that is able to echo much louder because of the extra space in my mouth... *HA HA HA*! My Gap is a daily affirmation that I am intelligent, beautiful, and LOVED. There is no question—only abundance of the emotional, spiritual, and monetary sort is going to come my way to fill all that space supported in radical self-love.

Ase.

MADIHA KHAN

Over the past few years, I've reclaimed my body in different ways. This has been fighting for the right to documentation, learning to appreciate my body throughout its many changes, and appreciating my accomplishments and progress within it. Recently, I was in a situation where someone was trying to make me feel as if my body wasn't mine, and I believed it. I allowed my body to face violence despite all the growth I had achieved and succumbed to another person's control. I eventually released myself, but I was still upset at myself for allowing my family to guilt me into keeping my body from its goals and passions for the sake of cultural appearances. The incident within this story stayed within me for months, and I knew I had to let it out. I knew I had to appreciate the struggle I overcame and I had to make a declaration. This piece is a declaration and reminder to myself that I have survived through the worst experiences of my life by choosing myself. In continuing to do so, my growth will not cease.

**SCAN TO
WATCH A LIVE
PERFORMANCE
OF THE PIECE.**

CHOOSING ME

Ammi. You were supposed to by my world, the cocoon in which I could wrap myself in, the protector you convinced me you were.

It's a late Friday afternoon. I drop you off at the ever-popular SoCal outlet mall after you decide I look like shit and need new clothes. I waited for about two hours until you get back: *"Dekho mein tumhare kill ye kitna kam karthi hoon. Eese lardki se kon shaadi kaare ga?"* Look how much effort I put into you. Who's going to marry someone like you?

As we get back on the street, I mumble back something I know will make you angry as I'm too emotionally exhausted to take the high road.

Imagine my surprise when you curled your hand into a fist and socked me from the passenger seat. Let me remind you, I'm driving! Shaking, I try to work through the shock of what happened and try to get us both home safely. Home. The place you were supposed to be for me, where the abundant love you proclaimed to have contrasted with every word and action you directed my way.

You continued screaming at me, saying that I made you do it. If I would just behave and listen to you, I wouldn't bring out the worst in you.

You waited for me to speak and my silence angered you more. You couldn't control your rage and, before I could react, grabbed my steering wheel and yanked it to the right and the left. The cars in the other lane swerved into the shoulder to avoid crashing into us.

WHAT THE FUCK IS WRONG WITH YOU, PAAGLE HE KYA? *"Are you insane?"*

I don't know how we avoided a 3-car crash but I tried to keep my composure in between my crying, shaking hands, and quivering body. I need to pack my bags and get the fuck out of here. I sped until I parked into our driveway, still crying out loud. I ran to my childhood room where I remembered you stabbed my pillow pet with a kitchen knife, because you were upset that my boyfriend gave it to me. I thought to leave, but I worried for my dad.

That night, I moved the sofas from the living room behind my door as I found out you had keys to my bedroom lock. Weird, right? I thought so too.

The next morning, you demanded I drive you somewhere. For fear of my safety, I refused. You circled my bed and tried to convince me that whatever happened the day before was no big deal, that I was being dramatic, that it was all in my head. As I refused and asked you to leave, I saw another fist forming but this time knew what to do. As I raised my hands to defend myself, you got angrier.

"How dare you raise your hands at me!?"

"I'm protecting myself!"

This was humiliating, this was dehumanizing. I was expected to take the beating. I tried to defend myself. I didn't want to fight my mother, I just wanted to get away from her. You pulled at my hair and scratched my arms. As I tried to get away from under you, you forced your arm over my throat and pressed it downwards. I couldn't breathe. I thought you, the person who brought breath into me, were going to take it away.

"How dare you? You did this. You deserve this."

Scared for my life, I kicked you to escape, and ran out of the house, and drove back to the Bay shortly after. After I left, you and dad left many voicemails on my phone.

"Stop being childish. You're becoming too American, these Gorei values have

changed you."

The worst were, *"Proper Pakistanis listen to their parents. It's not abnormal to hit your children. You've grown soft,"* and, *"If you come back, I'll forgive you for what happened."*

If you check the National Domestic Violence Hotline, it offers many reasons why we don't leave abusive relationships. I realized I had normalized my abuse to living in an immigrant household and held a lot of shame. As a South Asian person, I've heard so many renditions of abuse normalized in our households: Russel Peters' *"Somebudys gonna get a hurtin'"* or peers telling me, *"Yes, my mom also used to hit me with a coat hanger."* This is wrong.

I had chosen my family over myself for too many years and this time, I chose myself. Mom, I'm no longer willing to risk my safety for the sake of keeping up cultural appearances or whatever it is you use to justify your actions. I still love you and appreciate you for all that you've done, but this is my body, and I can't let you hold power over it any longer.

This is my body. It is safe, confident, self assured, a little clumsy, often a little kooky, and not any less Pakistani because it cut its hair, got a septum, or ran away from violence. This is my body, and it is its own protector.

LULU CHENG

It's funny now to look back and think that I almost decided not to perform. Like many women, I have a complicated relationship with my body. The idea of getting up on stage in front of loved ones and strangers alike, to talk about this deeply personal and vulnerable thing, was daunting. This is something that I think about every day, but rarely talk about with other people.

The turning point was when I realized that I was in the driver's seat. I could control exactly how much I wanted to share with the audience, and the messages I wanted them to walk away with. I didn't have to perform my pain for others. It sounds obvious in hindsight, but it was a journey to get there.

One of the best things that's happened as a result of the performance is the conversations it has sparked with friends and family. I feel more supported by and connected to them than I ever have before. A lot of what makes vulnerable topics hard is the lack of community and dialogue around them. If sharing my story can play a small part in changing that, that makes me really happy.

**SCAN TO
WATCH A LIVE
PERFORMANCE
OF THE PIECE.**

THE FIRST RULE
OF BEING THIN

The first rule about being thin is that you don't talk about being thin. Other people can talk about your body, of course:

- "你太瘦了, 要多吃一点!"
- *"You're too skinny, eat more!"*
- *"I wish I could eat anything and still be thin."*
- *"Everything looks good on you because you're skinny."*

When people make these comments, the only acceptable response is to look down and smile graciously, as if you've been given a gift.

Thin privilege is a seductive gift. There's the ex who had a habit of complimenting my body as if it was the highlight of the relationship. The friend who nods knowingly when she sees I've ordered a salad and says, *"That's why I'll never be skinny, I don't have your self-control."*

So you take the gifts and you set them aside and you try to forget about them. It's not like they mean anything, they're just things well-intentioned people say. It's not like, after hearing these comments over and over, you might become attached to the ideals, to the beauty standards they represent. It's not like gift boxes ever turn into cages.

Accumulate, verb: To gather together or acquire an increasing number of.

What do we accumulate in a life? Things, memories, pounds, identities.

Marie Kondo says to let go of things that no longer bring you joy. But what if the thing you're trying to let go of is an identity you didn't ask for, never realized you valued, until it started to slip away? Until you could no longer take it for granted. Until you started to lean on food for emotional support.

How do you say goodbye to an identity that's so universally rewarded in our culture? How do you say goodbye to an identity that has hooked itself into every aspect of your life? What you eat, how you eat, what you wear, how you move, the way you socialize, the things you notice about other women, the way you feel about yourself.

Here's what I do know: I am angry.

Angry that I bought our culture's lie that controlling a number on a scale means that I have control over my body. That this would keep it safe from other people's judgement.

Angry about all the time I've wasted thinking about something as superficial, and as consequential, as my weight.

Angry about how all that energy could have gone into other things, like writing poetry and learning how to cook, and enjoying the company of people I love.

Angry enough to want reparations from the media, from family members and friends and coworkers and exes and strangers—from everyone who's knowingly or complicitly reinforced harmful expectations of female beauty.

And I'm angry with myself. For not being strong enough to push back on those expectations. For not being able to separate my self worth from how much I weigh. For not being able to not care.

Buried in the middle of this anger, is slow, slow healing. I'm learning how to recognize unwanted gifts. I'm trying to surround myself with people who celebrate the qualities in me that I want to stand for.

I'm not sure I'll ever be free of the daily negotiation, the constant battle between honoring my body and yielding to someone else's expectation. But I can try to nurture new identities that might grow stronger than the old vines, that might one day make the bars of this cage a distant memory.

BRITTANY RAE BUCKMIRE

In thinking about my body I began to seriously consider the gulf between my inner life and my daily external performance of self. That questioning led me to think more critically about my relationship to race, its performance, and how I've used voice as a tool to assimilate and adapt to different environments; how language has been used as a weapon and a shield at different points of my life.

Peeling back these layers felt vulnerable because I didn't know what I'd find beneath them. I've been performing so long I wasn't sure who I was when no one was watching or who I'd be in a world beyond race, where I wasn't defined by what I was or wasn't, but could just be. And that's when I realized that the answer could be found by returning to nature—that I could reconnect to a truer sense of self by finding my roots, brown toes kissing brown earth.

I'm still grappling with how to use my voice authentically and unapologetically regardless of context. That work has only just begun, but this story was my entry point for inquiry and healing and I'm so excited to share it with you!

**SCAN TO
WATCH A LIVE
PERFORMANCE
OF THE PIECE.**

TRILINGUAL

I learned my first language in the shaded corner of a schoolyard.

"Why do you talk white?"

The words fall from her full lips between loud smacks of Bubble Yum gum and hang heavy in the air above my head.

"No, I don't!"

"Yes you do!," she claps back as she shifts her weight to sit in her hip and snakes her chin forward, a challenge.

I look around to the other girls who have gathered, eyes pleading for someone to come to my defense and when I see six sets of puzzled eyes looking back at me, I realize that this is not only a challenge, it's a trial.

"No I..." I trail off into silence equal parts a prayer for the miracle of invisibility and also for the sudden gift of street cred.

Sandra pops her gum, waiting. These girls really want an answer and I'm still scrambling to find it when, by the Grace of the Grade School Gods, the bell rings and just like that recess comes to an abrupt end. The girls lose interest and turn their backs on me, classroom bound, but I can't move. Feet heavy, pin pricks stinging behind my eyes.

Never let them see you cry.

"Yo, girl, you mad funny!"

"Yo, girl, you mad funny!"

"Yo, girl, you mad funny!"

As with mastering any language, I studied the native speakers, practiced their cool confidence and Philly attitude. I learned to leave letters hangin' off the ends of words, seasoned sentences with flavors that floated through my bedroom window at night and began to perform speech the way they thought a black girl should.

Then when I was nine, my landscape changed. My mom got a new job so we packed up our things and moved from the heart of Philadelphia to an apartment on the edge of a farm, trading high rises for horses, city streets for ambling creeks. But the biggest trade we made? Leaving our colorful community for a token existence as one of only a handful of black families in the town. In this new world, I went from not being black enough to being seen only as black. Moved from misunderstanding to misunderstanding, from outsider to other.

•

"Calm down, there is no need to yell or get upset."

That soft, White Lady voice they use every time they think I'm stepping out of my lane. A tone that mocks: "See how crazy and angry you sound compared to my slow and condescending diction?"

"I'm not yelling."

"The teachers...Well, we've been talking and we think you may have some anger issues."

Angry, overly dramatic, crazy, volatile. These are the labels that get attached to my dark skin and strong voice in white spaces. Labels to remind me that my dark skin disqualifies me from the privilege of expression without consequence and caution me to speak carefully in mixed company, to hold my tongue until it aches to hold it any longer.

These labels are part of a bigger strategy to put me into a box that reads "Caution: Angry Black Woman." This box is centuries old, crafted by fear and sanded smooth by ignorance. These are the walls that I've been fighting against from my first day of third grade when I became "the Black girl." Walls built for the sole purpose of distorting, dismissing, undermining, and flattening my whole person into trope because I dare to use my voice.

But of course I didn't know this in the third grade. All I knew was that I seemed to always find myself in trouble at school for what was, to me, no good reason. No matter what my intention was, it seemed like I was always misunderstood or not heard, so I adapted and learned my second language. I studied how to make myself mirror again, this time projecting a different image. I learned it was easier for them to see me as whole if they heard themselves in me. I believed that if I thought twice before I spoke, they'd think twice before putting me in that box. I came to understand that in white spaces what you say is often less important than what you don't.

Don't say anything when they put their hands in your hair.

Laugh along when they call you Oreo: black on the outside, white on the inside.

Smile after they tell you that you're not one of those black people, you're different.

Stay silent when your boyfriend tells you his friends asked if you taste different.

Don't break the silence about violence against black bodies at the hands of the state.

Remember always that you are equally invisible and hyper visible, always watched and held to a different code of conduct.

This second language developed and followed me from third grade to my corporate desk, ingrained and reinforced every time I found myself fighting against the tight walls of that box.

•

I was minding my own business with my whiskey ginger and my two step on the dance floor when a couple of white guys approached me to start a dance battle. It was my first year in San Francisco, a city with its own complicated relationship to race. I was with a group of mostly white co-workers and decided it was easier to play along than cause a scene. So I fought a heavy eye roll and took a sip of my drink to wash down the impending discomfort and cringe.

I know I'm just a prop for their entertainment. A souvenir story they'll tell over brunch tomorrow, and she knew it too as she broke through the crowd that had gathered, reached for me, and whispered loud above the music, "*You don't have to do this!*"

It was one of those time stands still moments. This woman I've never seen in my life has just read me. Seen right through the act. She was gone as quickly as she came, but her words stuck with me.

On the way home, I reflected on my lifetime of performing race. I thought about DuBois' words about, "feel[ing]... two-ness,—an American, a Negro; two souls, two thoughts, two unreconciled strivings; two warring ideals in one dark body." He coined this double consciousness, but as my Uber glided across the Bay Bridge I wondered if there is a third consciousness? A true self that is bigger and more complex than "American" or "Negro." A space beyond the construct of race, where you can fully embrace your place on the broad spectrum of Blackness but not be defined by it. I was tired of acting, performing, code switching, gum popping, tongue holding, box resisting. I was tired.

My weariness led me to learn my third language. In cultivating my relationship with nature and the outdoors, I have found solace from the stage. I've learned my greatest lessons from studying the trees. They stand their ground, no matter the terrain, no matter who happens to walk by. Rooted firmly into the earth, connected to and supported by their forest of ancestors. Unapologetically themselves in their dark-brown bark and halo of leaves, they have given me the gift of me. Getting to know my self a little deeper through getting to know this earth has helped me shed the notion that I need to be something other than myself because what I am isn't enough. I am bigger than Black. I am bigger than White. A woman of two worlds but a daughter of the earth.

The next time someone asks me, "*Why do you speak white?*" I'll simply look at them, stand a little taller and reply, "*I don't talk white. I speak trees.*"

LAUREN ITO

Writing and performing this piece was a journey of untangling knots. Six months after moving to San Francisco, I experienced a racially-motivated hate crime in Golden Gate Park. The experience left me mentally and emotionally depleted, while simultaneously confronted with fundamental questions about my identity. *Who am I? Who does society assume I am? What are the consequences of those assumptions? How do I redefine safety in a system that was not designed to love someone who looks like me?* In the process of reconciling, acknowledging, and pushing back against these questions, I connected with writing as a medium to heal.

This piece is a love letter to myself and my community. It is a reminder we can always rewrite the narratives we've inherited in a language of our choosing.

**SCAN TO
WATCH A LIVE
PERFORMANCE
OF THE PIECE.**

THIS STORY IS FOR YOU

The stranger's face was like sunken, tattered leather. White hate swings from beneath a baseball cap. Lessons learned that day:

1. Words burn holes through bellies.
2. When he says, "*Shut the fuck up you chink-ass bitch*"—believe him, he means it.
3. Monsters don't lurk in the shadows. They bask in the sun rays of Golden Gate Park at 2:00 p.m. on a Saturday.
4. Rearing up like a snake ready to strike he says, "*Go back to your country! If you don't get out I'll make you get out*"—brace for impact.
5. 10 minutes feel like 10 lifetimes as he follows you. He'll breathe daggers down each vertebrae stitching your body together as legs fly anywhere but here. Anywhere but here.

During said ten minutes, my body was hungry. Eyes starved and scavenging for sticks, rocks, stones, anything to defend myself...but none of which were to be found. Hungry eyes finally spot a giant log and you'll think, "*Almost... really? Fuck.*"

Yes, it was scary—all of it. But that's not what I remember the most. Even after he was swallowed by San Francisco wildflowers, his hatred remained hot at your heels. His hatred hot at your heels follows you home. Seeps under the door. Suffocates you as your body trembles, rocking...curled against the wall on your bedroom floor.

You'd repeat:

"*What does this mean? What does this mean?*" a question that really asked:

"Why after five generations in this country can we still never belong?"

Lessons learned in that day's wake:

1. The white policeman and white policewoman, privilege shimmering across porcelain skin, have been bred to blame you.
   a. They'll ask, *"What did you do to provoke this man?"*
   b. They'll ask, *"Could you have been doing anything to instigate this?"*
   c. They'll ask, *"Were you walking anywhere in the park you shouldn't have been?"*
2. Lectures are given without permission to those who cannot fend for themselves because, *"As a small girl new to a big city you really need to be more aware of your surroundings and prioritize your safety."*
3. Five asks to file a police report will be met with a *"No"* by the mouth of an officer who knows it's illegal. *"I don't believe this was a hate crime,"* turns mantra affirmed over and over until he who proclaims it knows it to be true.
4. You'll learn those entrusted to protect your rights walk all over them saying *"I'm not belittling you do you hear me? I'm not belittling you."*
5. Your body can churn with raging emptiness. Your body can sit on the floor of the shower, water scalding skin not knowing whether or not you're even crying.

Some days my mom says, *"The past is in the past."* Other days my dad says, *"To know who you are, you must know where you come from."*

We are here. Five generations on this soil and still finding our way back home.

My great, great grandparents came here by way of sugarcane, pulled by the promise of a better life. We've been chasing that promise ever since. You, this body, here, and now, my child. We exist because of them. Our ancestors tilled this earth tender before you were born. Excavated rocks on bent knee so you may blossom in this fertile soil.

Lessons learned in the aftermath

1. My body is resilient.
2. That which we carry we carry for a reason.
3. Sometimes it's a hate crime that shakes you awake.
4. The healers will come. They'll teach you, "*Tears do water the seeds of transformation within us.*"
5. We can always rewrite our own creation stories. I am rewriting my creation story. On this day, on this stage, love, this story is for you.

JADE-OLIVIA PATTON

I approached the writing of this part of my story in the way I approach most of my storytelling, which begins with the simplest step of reflecting on the event itself. When I began writing, I started off with just the facts. Everything else came into focus when I shifted my lens from the facts to perspective. I didn't completely realize the transformative nature of the process until I was almost done writing it and saw it completely come together from the details I'd added after the first version. I knew it was missing deeper substance and delving into that is where the real work happened. I had to go through the process of zooming out and zooming in to articulate the full scope of the story and how it affected my life, not just at that particular time, but my life in its entirety.

When I was writing this piece, I was at a point where I knew I had to confront this event. I knew it was toxic to allow it to be in my face and ignore it. It was a story I'd held internally and at a distance. It was a story I knew I would one day tell, but I'd always thought it would be much, much later in life. As if that would somehow give it less significance.

I arrived at a point where it was evident that my experience wasn't an isolated event that happened to me, but one that informed a lot about my being and traits of myself I hadn't recognized before. I entered a space where I was learning what I was truly made of and what that meant for the decisions I was making. While the core of this story is centrally focused on one event, it has many more layers that illustrate a culmination of experiences that have shaped my identity and the beliefs I hold pertaining to myself and others.

**SCAN TO
WATCH A LIVE
PERFORMANCE
OF THE PIECE.**

REHAB

This is my body
Laying on my bed
Asleep in my room
On familiar sheets
In my sanctuary
Out of my clothes
And in my skin
This is my home

I'm in undergrad and life is good. I'm living my best life years before it becomes a song.

What's this?

A girl who's been setup for a naked photo in her sleep, with a used condom placed on her body, with a fraternity shirt and bracelet AND the poster with her name on it from crossing her sorority? And it's been shared as a trophy. One to fifty to hundreds of people seeing it on GroupMe....this is sick and twisted.

Wait a minute. What does that say? THAT'S MY NAME.

As I view this very image on a phone that I never knew was being taken and never gave permission to exist I am experiencing this invasion of my home.

This is my body
Laying on my bed
Asleep in my room

On familiar sheets
In my sanctuary
Out of my clothes
And in my skin
This is my home

That is my comfort zone being desecrated in what seems to be live action. My sacred space, and it's been exposed to the world that is our college campus. And I'm not the only one viewing this image.

Because in this age of rising technology usage, news of home invasions spreads rapidly without means to an end. Everyone's got it but no one knows where it came from.

I do.

It was you.

You who came here with a plan
To get a lay of the land
To steal my sense of security
To take advantage of my innocence
To disrupt my sphere of comfort
To dismantle any semblance of trust
And to leave with satisfaction
Quietly, yet unmistakably so.

But this isn't about you.

I have a disorder in my right leg that is painful when I'm stressed. The pain can be debilitating to the point where I'm unable to walk. This physical manifestation of stress was the reason I never saw myself participating in a range of activities like running.

Before deciding to move to the Bay, I look around and I am tired. Tired of living in this tiny, little existence of a life I have stuffed into the corners of the city of my alma mater in which I remained after I graduated. Where I would run into old classmates randomly from time to time, feeling the shooting pain up my right leg for an instant. *Stressed.*

Did they see that photo? What are they thinking of me? Will they mention it?

I ache of social anxiety and exposure where I want to make myself disappear and would rather hide in the house than to confront the remembrance of shame.

But the decision of relocating across the country gives me permission to shed this shame and come out of hiding. This is my fresh start.

Or so I thought.

When I moved to the Bay in the summer of 2018, I felt I was "home free" until I was unexpectedly triggered by that traumatic home invasion from so many years before. It all came flooding back when I realized I had moved to the same city where he was from and now living as well.

But because of this news I know this is a sign that this is my time. My time to resolve to override the physical pain in my body. The undoing of years of silence. The rebuilding of my self-worth. This is it.

So I take to the pavement. Something I've never done before, something I never even dreamt of doing. I decide to start running. One foot at a time. Left foot, right foot. *Pain.* Left foot, right foot. *AH!* Until I am pounding the pavement, crushing the concrete beneath my feet which feels like crumbling the hold humiliation had on me.

I remember those words being said to me:

"Drop it, Jade. You took this too far. It wasn't that serious. Everybody slips up."

Left foot, right foot, left foot.

"You'll be fine. Is letting it go not an option?"

Left foot, right foot, *pain*.

"Females are emotionally unstable."

Left foot, right foot, left.

"I thought you'd drop it by now."

Left foot, right foot.

Remembering the bile rising in my throat the moment he walked into my health class mid May and the dizziness that ensued as I managed to escape that building before tears burst through after realizing I had been holding my breath the entire time.

Left foot, right foot, *pain*.

Retelling my story to one detective, then the next, and the next. Reliving every detail, recalling all of the things I want to not be real.

Left foot, right foot.

I hear the words, *"The court of law finds you guilty,"* and find temporary relief that some justice has now been served.

Left foot, right foot.

Beating the betrayal of those who turned their backs in crude judgment of me in my darkest hour. Erasing regret, rage, and resentment, and finding release. This is a renovation of my home. The restoration of me.

Left foot, right foot.

As the pounds melt off my body so does the heaviness of hiding, the guilt and disgust, the sickness of shame, and so comes forgiveness and fortitude.

On January 13, 2019, I completed my first 5k. I ran Golden Gate Park without stopping, one foot at a time, just like I'd practiced, but this time with friends at my side, and belief that I could do so. Up until that day I'd only been able to run for 12 minutes straight. On that day I ran for 37 minutes and 53 seconds. It was beyond freeing. A "runner's high" can't even begin to describe the euphoria that came over my body as I approached that finish line.

•

I feel the rain pouring down on my face and I cannot tell the difference between it and my tears flowing freely. I inhale deeply and exhale slowly, freeing my breath, running to and no longer running from.

This is my body
Laying on my bed
Asleep in my room
On familiar sheets
In my sanctuary
Out of my clothes
And in my skin
This is STILL my home.

KIERA A.

One of my goals for 2019 has been to force myself out of my comfort zone and one of the ways I intend to do that is through writing. The opportunity to write a piece and take the time and space to share it on stage forced me to be vulnerable in new ways.

At the time that this piece was composed, I was incredibly overwhelmed and feeling capable of only going through the motions of life, continuing to show up where I was expected to but neglecting my well being in the process. This piece illustrates the stress I was covering up each day but unable to separate myself from.

**SCAN TO
WATCH A LIVE
PERFORMANCE
OF THE PIECE.**

HOW I CARRY MYSELF VERSUS WHAT I CARRY

This is the body of a pole dancer. I have a corporate job, but pole dancing is what I do in my free time. It's become my stress reliever, my mood lifter, my escape.

My dancing vocabulary has grown so much since I started.

Arching, rising, leaping, rolling, twirling, spinning...

Dancing has brought me a new confidence, a sense of liberation. It's taught me to live comfortably in my decisions, to feel empowered in being unapologetic.

I am always so proud to be on stage dancing. It's fun to show off what I know, the challenging moves I've conquered, the pretty shapes my body can make.

One of my instructors pointed out, "*I love watching you dance because that's when you stop thinking and you're just... free.*"

Tuh. Funny you say that.

•

Very recently, I learned what imposter syndrome is. I've long been familiar with the term, but I only recently learned what it means.

In the past few months, I received a stellar recommendation from a person I admire, I started exploring opportunities I otherwise wouldn't have thought myself qualified for, I was promoted at work, and I've really started to see my "tribe" come together.

In the midst of all these experiences, I have been so supported by my friends, my family, and my coworkers who were each genuinely excited by the things I was sharing with them.

But I was much less excited. What each of these experiences meant for me was anxiety, a hell of a lot of overthinking.

My mind stuck, spinning on the same thoughts. Over and over and over again.

Hours spent discussing my doubts with myself.
Fatigue, and a lot less sleep.
Bad dreams if I did sleep.
Lost appetite.
Migraines for days on end.
Tears.
Most notably, Stress-induced rashes.

•

Through all of the compliments and congratulations, I was feeling immense pressure to maintain as the strong, confident, poised person everyone knows me to be.

I felt like I couldn't mess up. For all the asks for support, referrals, recommendations, advice, I felt like I had to execute.

I wanted to show the people around me that they didn't waste their energy on me.

When I think about it, it makes me itch.

•

As if I had never written or spoken before, I felt incapable of composing myself to see any task through. I spent hours at a time questioning myself. *Who would support me in this? Am I qualified? Do I even deserve this? No. Maybe it's not for me.*

I was counting myself out.

I feel so blessed to have experienced all the opportunities that have been set in front of me. And I hate to admit it, but the anxiety that came along with this apparent season of fruitfulness was paralyzing.

Maintaining my composure means keeping what's inside in. Meanwhile, my body is undergoing such trauma. Reaching to extremes, manifesting physically, pleading with me to seek freedom.

LET. IT. OUT.

•

I often ask myself is all this stress worth it? Does it serve me?

There's something I didn't tell you about earlier. When I was changing into my dance clothes, my hand brushed by my stomach and I paused in front of the mirror.

A rash has appeared there, too. It crept from the tops of my feet up to my thighs. Wrapped around my stomach and hips. Crawled up my sides and back...

I thought, *"Good thing I don't have to climb or invert today."* That means I don't need to have skin exposed and I can dance in full leggings and sleeves.

Again, I ask, *"Was all the stress worth it?"*

Not only had it found a way to creep into my corner of freedom, marrying the thing I enjoy the most with the thing I could most do without, none of those opportunities I was obsessing over worked out as I expected them to.

So I continue to ask myself, *"Does it serve me? Is all this stress worth it?"*

SHEMIKA LAMARE

When I wrote this piece, I started with the body hair that was easiest for me to accept and progressed from there. It was difficult choosing which body hair stories to highlight, but after some feedback from my first draft I realized I wasn't telling the *real* story. I wasn't being vulnerable and this pushed me to tell stories that I had never shared with anyone before. I chose this story because I was at a point in my life where I no longer thought about my body hair. I had reached a new normal. Accepting my body hair has been a part of a larger journey. A decade ago, I started playing a *Game* with myself of asking *why* until I found the *real* reason. For example: *"Why am I shaving my legs?"* Because my sisters do it. *"Why?"* Because girls are supposed to. *"Why?"* Because societal expectations. *"Does that align with MY values?"* No.

Playing this *Game* with myself has helped me chip away at societal expectations and spend time figuring out my own views. It started with how I styled my hair, wore bras, and eventually built up to the products I use and whether the companies' values align with mine. The body hair *Game* is done, but I still have plenty of other *whys* I'm working on answering and adjusting to fit my values. There were so many other stories I could have told like my childhood, my scars, being a Black Woman in society, but body hair was the one story I had never heard. Sure I've seen other people with body hair, but I don't know their reasons or journey. I spent so many years aimlessly repeating a ritual of removing a piece of myself with no justification. Writing and performing this piece was a form of healing with the added benefit of being able to plant a seed in people's mind to think about their story.

**SCAN TO
WATCH A LIVE
PERFORMANCE
OF THE PIECE.**

THAT BODY

THIS wasn't always MY BODY.
Then, whose body was it?

Well. A mix. ⅓ my family views, ⅔ peer pressure, and a heavy, HEAVY dose of the media; basically, one body full of internalized views from society.

That Body.

That body was 11 years old when she went to that AWKWARD...very AWKWARD middle school assembly. The one where boys and girls are sent to separate rooms to watch that cringe-worthy video about hormones, body hair, and periods.

That body had gotten its period and was feeling like a young lady. Prickly hairs had began forming, taking over what used to be a smooth skin. Shaving felt like a rite of passage into womanhood, at least that's what it SEEMED like.

That Body, it grew into a 20-something-year-old who rarely shaved her legs out of pure laziness.
But was I lazy?
Or was it that I finally noticed the gendered double standard that our society pushes.
A man can have all the hair.
But a woman, you know the SAME species, is expected to be hairless?
Make it make sense.

Not only is shaving emotionally taxing, it's costly.
When I was creating my budget, I realized that I was about to spend $240 a
year to get my eyebrows done.
Why was I going to spend money on trying to get fleeky eyebrows?
Issa no!
It was easy to stop cold turkey because I never consistently got them done.
I always viewed them as an enhancement of my beauty never a necessity.

Prickly leg hair and bushy eyebrows.
Now what you've really all been wondering is:
What about her VAGINA?
Her pussycat? Her coochie? You know, "down there?"
No, I don't shave my vagina.

Actually were y'all even wondering about my coochie hair?
Or was it the internalized views from society that I had ingested which made
me think, that's what everyone was wondering.
Or was it teenage Shemika that had seen *Scary Movie* (the funny one)?
Where the guy spends a few minutes trying to cut, dive, finagle his way
through a women's pubic hair.
Or maybe it's the silence.
The not-so-talked-about pubic hair ONLY ever discussed in reference
to removal.

**These experiences lead me to feel insecure when I decided to bare my full
"bush" to my first partner.**
But that partner and the partners to come were NEVER concerned with it.
It made think it was another gendered double standard, where women felt
one way, but men never actually cared.

Prickly leg hair and bushy eyebrows, full vagina bush.
Now I struggled the most with letting my armpit hair grow.
As a black woman in San Francisco I already get stared at a lot.
I wasn't trying to bring more attention to myself.
Eventually, I caved after seeing a woman in dance class dancing carefree,

armpit hair and all.

Little did I know she was the representation I needed so that I could stand in my truth.

Three years fully hairy, I realize.
The questions that had always lingered were:
WHY am I shaving? (rite of passage my ass)
It's going to grow back, why bother?
Why was I going against what my body wanted to do?
It. wants. to. grow. hair.

Who knew it was a radical act to love myself, my body, as I am?

People still stare at my body hair.
And it may make THEM uncomfortable.
That's for them to reconcile with themselves.

I realize that the battle is far from over.
For now, I'm happy to acknowledge the GROWTH.
My body hair has helped me rediscover what it is to be me and in my body.
It's taught me to stand my ground;
To question why and how I am adhering to societal standards that I NEVER signed up for.

THAT body has grown into THIS body.
This body. A mix. ⅓ Fuck-It, ⅔ Self-Acceptance, and a heavy, HEAVY dose of Self-Love.

I am Enough. AS I AM.

This, this is MY body.

MAREKO PRIOR

Sometimes my attention to detail nudges me towards perfectionism. If there is a perfect version of a project, that's the ideal I work toward. I've only recently built comfort in sharing early, error-filled, or shaky drafts instead of just final, glossy products. So when I found myself (once again) skipping an event I'd been excited about because my hair was a mess, I blamed perfectionism for not getting myself out the door. And I felt horrible about it. That week I heard about *this is my body* and realized I had a story I wanted to tell.

The process of writing forced me to explore why I was judging myself against standards I would never set for anyone else. *If I don't look down at strangers with hair like mine that day, why did I have so much anxiety? What if perfectionism wasn't the issue?* That process, and openly talking about it with my castmates led to the insight I shared in "Specialized." This is a story happening now and one that's still unfolding. I'm not sure how this will all end yet, but I am proud of sharing this working draft of my bigger story.

SCAN TO
WATCH A LIVE
PERFORMANCE
OF THE PIECE.

SPECIALIZED

I'm special.
(But I know you can tell that just by looking at me.)

I figured this out pretty early. I'm biracial, was raised by my white mom and family and was one of the few people of color in the neighborhood.

So I was pretty young when I realized my skin was special.

For one, it changed colors. It soaked up the sun so quickly that after playing outside all day, I was a completely different color than I was at the start.

Now I know this isn't that big of a deal for many—just wear sunscreen, be careful of things that will give you weird tan lines. I watched my mom, and tried the same skin routines she did, but my skin came with needs that couldn't be met in the same way as hers.

And it invited constant feedback:
We went outside at the same time—I can't believe you already have tan lines! I wish I could get tan like you.
You're getting so dark! Be careful, you're light skinned so you don't want to get too much darker..."
It's crazy how much lighter you are in winter than summer!"

There's something about getting unsolicited feedback from friends, family, and strangers all the damn time—none of which your family ever gets, by the way—that makes you feel... special.

Not to mention all the times this special skin invited workers to follow me around in stores or ignore me at the counters—at least until they saw me rejoin my white family or address one woman as "mom." But that's a story for another day...

Because this body only got more special over the years. Puberty gifted me height and size 11 feet, just like my mom. And although it meant I could find shoes in her closet that fit, finding 11s in a store wasn't so easy. So few size-11 shoes were made that the rare pair usually had a bright yellow sticker on them.

I admit that it made shopping faster. Just look for yellow first and then worry about the style. Because looking for styles I liked usually came with, "*It's not in my size,*" or, "*We're out of stock here,*" disappointment.

That became especially true when I started gaining weight. Shopping got even faster. I didn't need to bother combing the racks looking for a yellow sticker. Now I got my own section. Usually "plus size" or "women's wear..." a section always separated from and rarely as big (ironically enough) as the one for normal women.

I started realizing that I was not just "the only one like me in the family," special, but "I'm not your target customer so you don't make as many products for me" special.

Not quite a "You need something custom-made" special, but definitely a "You need a special label or section," and "It's not exactly what you want, but take it because it's as close as you can get" kind of special.

And then there's my hair.

I love my hair. Love that it's naturally curly and big, but there's always so much I don't know:

"*I don't know why it takes me so much longer to wash my hair than yours.*"
"*I don't know why mine looks so different. I used the same products and methods*

as you did, but now it's dry and matted."

"I don't know her. She's definitely a stranger. So I don't know why she just reached out and touched my hair like that. It happens a lot."

When I was young, my mom once took me to her hair salon for a cut. And there's nothing like being turned away because, *"We don't do ethnic hair here,"* to make you feel real special. Especially when the black salons weren't thrilled to see me either as, *"We don't do natural hair here."* So special...

So what do I do with this special body? Well, I do my homework.

I know which Target stores have a whole aisle for natural hair care products instead of just that little section at the end.

I know which shoe stores label their 11s and typically have more than a handful in stock. I know which clothing stores have "extended sizes" in styles I'd actually like.

Since in-store options are generally limited, I know where to find discounts to offset the shipping prices of the clothes and shoes I can only find online. I've learned to wear my hair down when walking in a salon for the first time to see if they look scared - and when to just stop my stylist from trying the "curly hair method they just learned" because it NEVER ends well.

What else do I do with this special body? I settle... I settle a lot.

I can't find ones I like and fit so I pretend that cute shoes or clothes isn't something I care about.

I sometimes go years between finding someone who can actually handle my hair. So when it's in a funky, growing out stage, I just pull it back and ignore that I feel most like myself when it's down.

I know how I want to look, and sometimes I just can't find enough specialty versions to make it possible. It gets exhausting. And demoralizing.

I don't want to live in fear of uniforms or coordinated outfits where everyone else is identical and I'm, "the closest match we could find."

I just want to go to a store to get what I need. And to try things on there. And not have to decide if I want to keep those pants that don't fit quite right, but...do I really want to take the time to mail them back? Or not get fully refunded for it because of "restock fees." Why do I have to pay just to try stuff on?

Being special has made it really hard to represent myself as I truly am, and not the version I settled for. I have days where I just don't go out. I've never left the parking lot at some events because I couldn't let this version of me walk through the door when it felt so disconnected from who I truly am. The average woman's clothing size is now between a 16 and a 18. There are over 5-million women in the US with size-11 feet.

I'm not that special.

And you should be able to tell just by looking at me.

SARAH D. PARK

It had been a while since I revisited this storyline in my life. I was curious to name how far I'd come so that I could move on from it. I had given lupus such power over my choices and my time for so long, and I was tired of letting that past still form me in my present. But as I tried to make room for new stories in my life, I realized that not talking about it also gave it undue power. I shared this story so that I could let it go.

**SCAN TO
WATCH A LIVE
PERFORMANCE
OF THE PIECE.**

WHO SAYS I'M FREE?

Take a good look at my body. How do I look? I look good, that's how I look! That's 'cause Asians don't raisin. Can you believe I'm 31? I look like I'm going to live forever. Or not.

You may not be able to guess, but there is a battle being waged inside my body. My body is actively fighting itself so much, I actually have to take meds to suppress its strength so that it doesn't hurt me.

You see, Western doctors have told me that I have a lifelong disease called lupus. My immune system is so overactive, it's attacking my kidneys, and so I have kidney disease as well. What that looks like is a lot of fatigue, and at some point, I'll eventually have to be hooked up to a machine to clean my blood for me or maybe receive a kidney from a stranger. The worst part of it is that it can happen in the span of a day or a long and happy life. I was 11 years old when they told me, barely starting life, and there is no cure.

This sobering picture of my future is an educated guess at what I could expect, based on countless other patients with my condition and what little research had been done. I began to live preventatively, making smaller choices because I couldn't afford the risk. And even the times I reached for the things that I wanted, my body would cut me down, grounding me when I wanted to fly—grounding me with depression, with shingles, with slivers of my kidneys being cut out to see how far they had failed.

That's a terrible story. I did not want this story. But this isn't the battle that I was referring to.

I also believe in a God who heals. All you have to do is ask. Sometimes, God says no, but sometimes, God says yes. I've heard the stories, and they're even written down. God offered a different story that involved a healing that could truly free me... from me.

Can you imagine?

I face two stories that are simultaneously true yet mutually contradicting. A life dependent on pills and a life dependent on God. A life of chronic illness and a life of promised freedom. And depending on which story I chose to believe, my body would bear the consequences.

There was one time, my doctors wanted to try a newly released treatment involving me stabbing my thighs with a needle every day for six months. I remember alternating my thighs so that it wouldn't bruise me too much.

Once, I received prayer at a charismatic church and the team that was praying over me said that they saw water washing over me. In faith, my family and I believed it and I stopped taking meds. Two months later, I'm holding clumps of my hair in my hands and holding back tears in my eyes, knowing I'd have to go back on meds again.

Honestly, it's much easier to believe in one story and make my peace with it, but with two? I'm dragging myself to refill pills again while dragging myself to the altar to pray for healing again, holding both most days. I used to save all my orange pill bottles in shoeboxes, waiting for the day I wouldn't need them anymore and burn them all in a toxic bonfire. But as I was collecting, the years collected as well—1, 2, 3, 4, 5, 6, 7, 8, 9, 10, 11, 12, 13, 14, 15, 16. This year makes 17. My closet's not that big, and I threw them all away.

And then, something new happened. Three years ago, my body became just stable enough where I could come off of meds completely. The doctors called it remission. My church called it a healing. I called it my freedom.

I could live life like a normal human being. Are you for real? Nothing to hold me back, but nothing to excuse me either, responsible for having the same shot at life as you.

It felt like getting away with something illegal! I could breathe deeply, time felt long, and anything was possible, because anything was possible. I quit my stable job, became an editor for a magazine, fell in love with that guy, moved to a beautiful city just because I wanted to. I cherished my failures, knowing that any mistakes I made wouldn't end up with me in a hospital. What a beautiful, finished story of God's goodness. I felt whole, complete, and ready to make up for lost time.

For one year. I got to know that freedom for one year.

In early March 2017, I noticed that my ankles were swollen. I watched in dismay as it spread up my legs, to my torso, even pillowing on my face and my fingers. If fluid was collecting in my tissues, then my kidneys were not properly working. Lupus was back.

But what a gift just a year without lupus has been! I got to explore it unencumbered, test what I was made of without anything holding me down. That year made freedom recognizable to me, enough to know that I still had such freedom when lupus came back, enough to continue in the choices I had made while still free.

I still felt free. What was the nature of this freedom, that I am back in the same circumstances that enslaved me—to drugs, fear, and precaution—but I still feel free?

I didn't see the need to move back home. My work was accommodating of my fatigue. I was able to have insurance that wasn't tied to any full-time job.

I always thought healing was complete freedom from meds, that I would have a new body taking care of me the way it was made to. But my friend Anne told me that healing can be defined in more ways than one; for some, healing is achieved when a person can resume living a normal life with the help of meds.

It's so obvious now, but why hadn't anyone told me? There is no language to bridge the body and the spirit, even thought it's all right here. My doctors delivered life-changing news but only dealt with the physical. And my faith does not know how to expand its definition of a miracle to include a pharmaceutical.

What if I had been free this entire time? What if I had been free this entire time? What if I had been free this entire time?

I am still free. I am still free. I am still free.

CLASSROOM GUIDE

PURPOSE AND SCOPE

this is my body is an anthology of written works by women of color exploring their relationship with their bodies in the world they exist in. The anthology is based on performance pieces in a show that supports individuals to explore their personal experiences within the context of society. Educators can use the pieces in the anthology to help students connect to a diverse range of voices, and write to connect their lives to themes within the curriculum.

GUIDING QUESTIONS FOR READING REFLECTIONS

- Which piece resonated with you, and why?
- What are some common themes that you see across the various pieces?
- How have some of the ideas shared changed, altered, or informed your perspective?

ACTIVITIES

- Encourage students to write a letter of appreciation to their body. What are they grateful for? What does it enable them to do? How does it make them who they are?
- Encourage students to write their own performance piece aligned to the main theme and provide the opportunity for them to share with another classmate or in the classroom setting.
- Align a piece to a theme you are teaching in your classroom. Ask students to engage in a discussion and conversation that discusses the piece.

FURTHER READING

BEAUTY STANDARDS

- "Beauty Gap by Brittney Enin
- "The First Rule of Being Thin" by Lulu Cheng
- "That Body" by Shemika Lamare
- "Specialized" by Mareko Prior

HEALTH

- "The First Rule of Being Thin" by Lulu Cheng
- "Rehab" by Jade-Olivia Patton
- "How I Carry Myself Versus What I Carry" by Kiera A.
- "Who Says I'm Free?" by Sarah D. Park

FAMILY

- "Choosing Me" by Madiha Khan
- "This Story is For You" by Lauren Ito
- "Specialized" by Mareko Prior

BELONGING

- "Beauty Gap" by Brittney Enin
- "Trilingual" by Brittany Rae Buckmire
- "This Story is For You" by Lauren Ito
- "How I Carry Myself Versus What I Carry" by Kiera A.
- "Specialized" by Mareko Prior

TRAUMA

- "Rehab" by Jade-Olivia Patton
- "Choosing Me" by Madiha Khan
- "This Story is For You" by Lauren Ito
- "Who Says I'm Free?" by Sarah D. Park

AUTHORS

KIERA A.

Friends and family describe Kiera as adventurous which is most apparent in the continuous leaps of faith she has taken throughout her life. The only person in her high school class to attend a historically Black university, Kiera moved 8 hours from home to enter a different world and experience Black culture in new ways. After graduation, the adventure continued when Kiera relocated to the Bay Area to begin her career as a marketer. Along the way, she picked up a creative hobby and is now an avid pole dancer.

Excited to challenge herself in her first ever solo performance, Kiera is looking forward to this new adventure and sharing of her experience in this year's presentation of "this is my body."

BRITTANY RAE BUCKMIRE

Brittany Rae is an Oakland-based storyteller finding expression and connection through writing, movement, and visual narratives. She is passionate about raising the voices and experiences of women of color and believes in the power of Black Girl Magic! Above all else, she is still becoming, unfolding, and exploring.

LULU CHENG

Lulu is a 1.5-generation "American Chinese," which she realizes sounds like a type of cheese. As a writer, illustrator, and performer, her work explores identity, the impact of technology, and human connection. She's passionate about helping people feel seen and more connected to one another, whether that's through amplifying underrepresented stories, teaching communication and relating skills, or building technology that promotes diversity and inclusion.

BRITTNEY ENIN

Brittney is the living Embodiment of #BlackWomanMagic. A recent Alumni of UC Berkeley, she radiates her purifying sunshine and radical positivity to those that come into her presence. She is an advocate for healing and social justice for marginalized peoples and aims to use her talent with words as well as her background in public health, to make a positive impact on her community. She is the founder of her own self-care consulting business where she empowers individuals and groups to get access to sustainable ways of living and access to Thriving. Now entering her 24th Sun-cycle of Life, she aims to bless the world with her words and kickstart her intention to become a writer and share her thoughts and ideas with the world.

LAUREN ITO

Lauren Ito is a gosei (fifth generation Japanese American) poet, photographer, and community craftswoman from an island outside Seattle. Her writing explores the tensions of choice and force within identity, inheritance, and home. Lauren's work has been featured by *The Seattle Times*, IDEO, National Japanese American Historical Society, the Japanese American Citizens League, and Bay Area Generations, as well as performance venues, including the Mission Arts Performance Project, Talk Story Oakland, and Gears Turning. She lives in San Francisco, and can almost always be found by the sea.

MADIHA KHAN

Madiha Khan is a "call you out on your bullshit" advocate, continuously learning to navigate the world and systems through the lens of her own intersectional identity. As a former undocumented individual, she is passionate in her work toward assisting others in developing their narratives and personal history to demand their human rights and liberation. Oddly, she also has intense stage-fright and is working toward developing her stage presence and confidence while relaying her narratives, working on herself, and (the hardest task) working on convincing her parents that women with short hair are badass. Madiha likes to lay down next to her two cats, eat super-spicy food, and vocalize the thoughts most people would keep to themselves.

SHEMIKA LAMARE

Shemika is a speaker, dancer, and is new to the world of improv. She enjoys immersing herself in the arts as part of her spiritual journey. She works at the intersection of Nonprofit and Tech. As a Data Scientist, she enjoys using data to gain insight and tell stories.

SARAH D. PARK

Sarah D. Park is a writer and performance artist whose work focuses on the cultivation of cross-racial dialogue with a Christian faith orientation. When she's not writing, she serves as a story producer for *Inheritance Magazine* and manages communications for Project Peace East Bay. Sarah graduated from Pomona College with a BA in Asian American Studies but realized she learns much better trying ideas out in life. She currently calls the Bay Area her home but is an Angeleno in appetite and a Korean American ahjumma at heart.

JADE-OLIVIA PATTON

Jade-Olivia is a native Detroiter and a fun-loving, energetic spirit who lives for good conversation and tear-inducing laughter. She's been a storyteller for The Stoop Storytelling Series in Baltimore and Spontaneous Storytelling at StorySlam Oakland. Known for her weekly Instagram story antics about the wonders of adulting in 2019 (#TrueLifeTuesdays and #WhatTheyWontTellYouWednesdays), she is determined to carve a path of her own through genuine social connections, acting, comedy, writing, improvisational theatre, and of course, storytelling.

MAREKO PRIOR

Mareko Prior is driven by service and fixated on access. She's committed to ensuring the likelihood of a young person's success in life isn't determined by their zip code. Specializing in mentorship and college access, Mareko uses her superpowers as an empath and connector to open the doors for her students to access the opportunities they deserve. The Chicago area, where Mareko is originally from, gave Mareko a slight accent, soft spot for deep dish, and refusal to call a "pop" a "soda." But her love for the city couldn't make up for the harsh winters there. Her decision to live an ice-scraper free life took Mareko to San Antonio, Texas, and now the Bay Area where she happily keeps her winter gear in storage. During down time she can generally be found in a movie theater, volunteering, preventing her craft projects from becoming "Pinterest-Fails," or writing.

EDITORS

VINA VO

Vina is a writer, consultant, and network builder who believes in the power of words to build bridges, heal wounds, and create new worlds. During her free time, she loves hiking, exploring new bookstores, meditating, practicing yoga, and cooking tasty meals. Above all, Vina consistently envisions a world where people can create their way to freedom. She is the co-founder of the Novalia Collective.

ODELIA YOUNGE

Odelia is an educator and writer based in Oakland, California. Odelia is the editor and co-author of the acclaimed *A FLY Girl's Guide to University: Being a Woman of Color at Cambridge and Other Institutions of Power and Elitism* (Verve Poetry Press, 2019). She has led work on transforming education, decolonising systems, and building out spaces for writers of color, while also organizing spaces for creative expression. Odelia is driven by her faith, radical black love, and the concept of creating yourself to freedom— forgetting what your oppressors have told you is the truth, and building anew. Odelia is the co-founder of Novalia Collective.

ACKNOWLEDGEMENTS

We are grateful for our family and friends who continue to encourage us on this creative journey. Thank you to J. K. Fowler and the Nomadic Press team for believing in our program and bringing it to life on the pages. Special thanks to Francois Cadieux, Michael Carpenter, Pastor Erna Hackett, Paige Mayes, Jesse Gurney, and Tyler Richendollar for supporting us in making *this is my body* an incredible process and experience. The program would also not be possible without those who donated so that every woman who wanted to take part in the show could be in the program. Most of all, we are grateful for the women who shared their lives and stories with us and the community.

ABOUT NOVALIA COLLECTIVE

We build spaces and opportunities for collective storytelling and community building. We work with both individuals and organizations to thoughtfully craft and design programs, initiatives, and strategic plans that work best for their business or community. We serve as partners who will be there every step of the way, asking all the hard questions, and obtaining desired results. Our team has over a decade of experience working across cultural and geographical differences to strengthen communities to connect, collaborate, and thrive. We have worked across the education, financial services, music, and environmental sectors to bring together stakeholders and decision-makers by organizing events, forums, and spaces for collective sense-making. Let's create ourselves to freedom together.

novaliacollective.com

 @novaliacollective

 /novalia collective